Home and College
by Frederic Dan Huntington

Address:
HardPress
8345 NW 66TH ST #2561
MIAMI FL 33166-2626
USA
Email: info@hardpress.net

Home and College

L. O. Lund

SIGILL: COLL: HARVARD: CANTAB: NOV: ANGL: 1650.
CHRISTO ECCLESIAE
VE RI TAS

Home and College.

~~~~~~~~~~~~~~~~~

A

PUBLIC ADDRESS

DELIVERED IN THE HALL OF THE

MASSACHUSETTS HOUSE OF REPRESENTATIVES,

March 8, 1860.

By F. D. HUNTINGTON,

PREACHER TO THE UNIVERSITY, AND PLUMMER PROFESSOR OF
CHRISTIAN MORALS IN HARVARD COLLEGE.

BOSTON:
CROSBY, NICHOLS, LEE, & CO.,
117 WASHINGTON STREET.
1860.

University Press, Cambridge:
Electrotyped and Printed by Welch, Bigelow, & Co.

HOME AND COLLEGE.

THE subject that I have been requested to bring before you, my friends and fellow-citizens, has been already announced in the notice that has called us together. It falls into place in a series of earnest inquiries as to the proper powers and methods of early education, and belongs especially to that department of this great theme which pertains to the Family. The precise question before us is this: What connection has the discipline of the child in his first years with his safety, success, and character in the public seminary, where he is sent to enter on the higher branches of scholarship ? Such seminaries are of different grades, names, and objects. The College may be taken as the representative of them all.

The statement of the question supposes that such an institution has a distinctive and easily recognized constitution; that the life lived in it is a peculiar kind of life, with its own forces and perils; and that certain conditions of honor, happiness, and usefulness are found there which justify a special consideration.

Of the College this is unquestionably true. More than most other forms of social living, it is a world within itself.

It has a local government; a characteristic public sentiment; a body of tradi-
tional notions, maxims, and usages, pure-
ly conventional, handed down from class
to class, and exerting an almost inevitable influence on every member. To a
great extent, unless favored by accidental
associations in the neighborhood, the students are removed from general society,
and for a large part of the year they are
with hardly anybody but each other.
They will have their own humors, fashions, politics, and prejudices. The com-
pactness of the population, the pride of
the place, and the quickness of youthful
sensibility, render them very sympathetic,
and sensitive to any impression affecting
their repute, passions, or interests; while

1 *

the moods produced are apt to be
changeable in proportion to their inten-
sity.` Of course, in such a spot, besides
the stimulus and the obstacles, the temptation and the support, common to humanity everywhere, there will be some
singular conditions of comfort, of enjoy-
ment, and of moral security and progress.

The other scene of culture that our
topic presents to us is the Family. This
is the primitive and simplest type of
social life. It is permanent and divine,
— an institution fraught with greater
blessings to man than any other beneath
the heavens, except the Church,— a nursery of the Church itself, and the chosen
symbol of the whole spiritual creation of
the Father. It was clearly the design

of the Maker of our manifold and marvellous organization that man should live in a Home. His faculties cannot unfold symmetrically and healthily save in its genial air, and amidst its varied and delicate system of dependencies, affections, amenities, and authorities. Something will always be wanting to the completeness of a character reared without this nurture, — some strength, or refinement, or other element of maturity. As civilization rises, the home grows sacred, becoming not only man's castle, but his conservatory, gallery, library, music-room, and oratory. With the school-house, the shop, and the sanctuary, it takes its place as one of the four representative structures of a cultivated and Christian state.

Marriage is its sacrament. Man in Christian wedlock, the house-band, is meant for its custodian, law-giver, instructor, and priest. Wise governments will watch scrupulously all specious invasions of its venerable and precious immunities to purity and order, — whether in the shape of a canting and corrupt polygamy assuming the pretence of religion, or of an arrogant and radical socialism, reasserting the license of nature, — and will take care to extinguish them by the imperative mercy of the law. Sensible and thoughtful people, acting in their individual freedom and responsibility, will resist all popular encroachments on the same great moral safeguard, whether these operate by letting children loose

into company and the street before their
principles can be formed, or by giving up every evening to public excitement, or by merging the reserved life
of the household in the promiscuous
eating-tables, vulgarizing mixtures, and
caravansary encampments of boarding-
hotels. Where would New England
have been to-day, if our fathers had
boarded out ? or had gone five nights in
a week to theatre and ball-room, with
perhaps a sacred concert and a lecture
on biology for the other two ? The
vigorous and muscular virtues of true
manhood and womanhood are nourished
and knit together, and made equal to the
pressure and soliciting of the world, only
by the wholesome retirement, and still-

ness, and meditation, and love, and faith of home.

Here, then, we have the two principal terms of our subject : College and Home. When the student goes to the College, he is separated temporarily from all domestic life, — not yet making his own home, leaving that of his childhood, and hanging between the two, in a state somewhat exceptional and unsheltered.

Various opinions are held by intelligent persons as to the desirableness and the moral effect of this absence from home. By the majority among us, it is probably regarded as simply a necessary means of getting at the benefits of the literary institution, with its expensive and rare apparatus, official staff, and scholarly appliances. That is, the arrangement is rather complied with than preferred. Others think it offers a positive advantage in the development of a youthful character. It is said to bring out self-reliance, balance, energy, tact, address; to break up inveterate and faulty habits in manners and temper; to rub off cobwebs, and smooth down angles; and so to do certain things for a young man, by way of enlarging and polishing him, which could not be done otherwise. This impression is very general in England, where it has contributed to the celebrity of the national schools and universities. So an eminent English scholar, in a popular work, I remember, represents a conceited

young lord as having an obstinate mass
of inherited arrogance and home-bred
nonsense taken out of him, on his first
arrival at Eton, by two timely kicks from
the son of a commoner, received on the
ball-ground. The same view prevails
considerably on the Continent, and is
held by not a few in our own country.
There is an obvious truth in it. But, in
general, the supposed advantage is occa-
sioned by some pre-existing defect or
mistake in the education or circumstances at home. Some passion has been
left uncurbed, some capacity neglected,
or some folly flourishing; and now the
best, if not the only, remedy is sought in
pushing off the wronged stripling upon
severer, or more exciting, or possibly
kindlier fortunes, among his fellows.

Directly opposite to this view is that which considers the removal of a boy from home, even for a limited period, to be a misfortune; and even suggests an attempt, as is now quite frequent, to break the force of that evil, by a temporary transfer of the family residence to the seat of the College.

Worse and more desperate than all is the custom, not altogether unknown, of sending the boy to College simply because he cannot be tolerated at home: as a convenient device for getting rid of his turbulent spirit, idle habits, and headstrong will, for four awkward years: making the institution, instead of his *Alma Mater*, — even should he survive the doubtful chances of matriculation, —

2

a sort of domestic Botany Bay for unruly children, where they do not *go*, but *are sent*, and where they do not stay, but are kept; and whence they are as apt to be rusticated as graduated. What effect this class of luxuriously-bred, pleasure-seeking, study-hating inmates are likely to have on the literary character, intellectual standards, and public reputation of a College, you can imagine.

There is, to be sure, a theory,— and in the nature of the case it can be at present little more than a theory,— that the College should make itself a substitute for the Home, cherish its children as under domestic influences, and stand toward them *in loco parentis*. We are told that college discipline should be fatherly and tender; that the students should be drawn into the families of their instructors, and should be admonished of their dangers, and corrected for their sins, as with the patient eye and hand and tongue of yearning affection. These are weighty words, and charged with solemn meaning. They will yet be spoken, and respoken, I trust, by lips of such authority, coupled with plans of such wisdom, in a time of riper Christian insight and attainment than ours, that they shall pronounce not only a prophecy, or a wish, but a blessed fulfilment and law. Meantime, however, it is right that it should be known where the real obstacle to such a confidential and delightful relation between pupil and teacher is to be found. It is not all on one side. It exists largely with the pupil himself and his friends at home. " To ask a college government to play the father to lads who have never learned what it is to be sons, is to make the place not only a Charity School, but a Foundling Hospital. Such a division of labor leaves the actual father only the right to indulge the child, and assigns to the Faculty the uncomfortable necessity of punishing him." Those parents who expect to take the benefit of a " paternal government" for their sons in the College must not make a mockery of it in their own habits. And the students themselves must entertain this pleasant theory of their relations *before* they are arraigned for violating the laws, as well as after. There are certainly some officers in all our Colleges that are not only ready, but eager, to welcome the members of their classes to their family circles, and to aid and support them with all the encouragements and counsels at their command. But on the student's part natural reserve, or the shyness created by an erroneous training, or an artificial notion of liberty, or a dread of stiff receptions, or a morbid pride of appearance, or the fear of being suspected of currying favor with the Faculty, stands in the way. And sometimes the very parents who have unconsciously prepared this result are the first to complain of it.

Indeed, as this last remark reminds us, one of the present embarrassments which attend our academic administration, and one which I gladly take this occasion to expose, is a too prevalent ignorance, if not a positive misunderstanding, on the part of the surrounding community, as to the actual interior spirit, life, and practical operation of our Colleges. I just spoke of these seminaries as little worlds within themselves. It is to be said, further, that they are worlds of which the community might advantageously acquire increased information. Gross misjudgments are continually coming to light as to the principles, the rules, and often as to the open facts of college government. In some cases, these false impressions only work out their damage in a private way. In others they get a public utterance, are circulated in the form of vague complaints, and perhaps furnish disparaging paragraphs for newspapers. But however held they exert an injurious influence on the institution, and, by weakening confidence in its management, abridge its usefulness. They tend to disturb, and, where there is already any excitement, to inflame and mislead the minds of the pupils, encouraging every little discontent or insubordination among them, and possibly tempting them into bolder acts of disobedience, which bring on heavier penalties. It would *seem* as if an extensive, established, responsible seat of

learning, largely directed by the representatives of the people, provided with
officers of ripe age, character, experience, and having no special motives to
abuse anybody or to hurt their own reputation, and acting as a check on one
another, might reasonably enough be
presumed to proceed in matters of education and discipline thoughtfully, con-
scientiously, tenderly, and wisely. It
would seem as if the occasional disaffec-
tion of a refractory or unsuccessful pupil might fail to justify a hasty censure,
whether in parlors or by the press. At
any rate, the liability to such misrep-
resentation would be much diminished
by a better acquaintance between the
outside of these institutions and the in-

side. They certainly need the moral support and reliance of right-minded men.
As with individuals, confidence in them
redoubles their power. They move on
in the best internal harmony, and to the
largest general benefaction, only when
the citizens in their homes comprehend
their policy, sustain their measures, and
are willing to bear some personal griev-
ances for the sake of their prosperity.

Be these things as they may, to the
College the young man comes. Time,
money, trouble, and anxiety are expend-
ed on his course. The first question is,
How shall that course be made honor-
able, happy, and successful ? How, for
the time while it is passing, and for the
future manhood ?

In answering this question, the primary sources to which we may look are three : the student himself, the institution that trains him, and the home that has trained him heretofore. Between these three parties the vast and august responsibility is divided.

Our concern, at present, is with the third ; — the one which is often left out of account altogether, as an indifferent or negative element ; the one which is very apt to forget that it has anything to do with the result. Parents look to their sons and to the College to achieve a result which their own mistakes have practically prohibited in advance ; or to correct faults which their own neglect has ineradicably planted ; or else to prune off excrescences which their own bad temper or taste has bound fast upon the boy's back, — the curse of his collegiate and all his after days. So far is this expectation from being just, that I suspect most college officers, who have been long in the habit of observing undergraduate developments of character, would be able to tell quite satisfactorily, before a class are half through their course, in what sort of homes the different members have lived, and to predict a result in accordance with that preparation.

For the sake of clearness and convenience, I shall take up a few of the characteristic features of the college experience, both as presenting points of peril and conditions of success, and ask you to look at them in order.

I. Let the first, because the most conspicuous of these, be the control of the appetites and animal passions. Not that sins in this regard are by any means the most deep-struck, subtle, or fatal of all moral disorders. Settled selfishness, cunning, deceit, and unbelief are all more hopeless. But sensual offences are visible and disastrous in their demonstration, quick in retribution, and in crowded populations, where the facilities of indulgence are multiplied, are frightfully fostered by social customs. Is it probable they will be originated at College, in a young man whose character has been free from them through his ear-

lier years ; where their germs have not
been suffered to form and grow ; where
habit has made self-control easy ; where
purity, of body and spirit, temperance in
· things allowable, and abstinence from
things· hurtful, have created a strong
vantage-ground, in the constitution, for
virtue ? Consider. The average age at
which Freshmen enter is now, perhaps,
eighteen years. Suppose it were a year
or two younger. Does it seem probable,
according to all we know of the moral
laws, that after that time, and within a
short period, desires which had before
been unfelt should break out into sudden
and ungovernable activity, or that those
which had been held in a rational sub-
jection should all at once overmaster

3

their restraints, and spring up with pru-
rient eagerness, and rush into shameless
license ? Allowing for exceptional instances, this would not be likely under
any circumstances : still less, where the
vigilance of governors, the rules of the
place, the standards of promotion, and
the exactions of daily routine in presence and study, all tend to resist propen-
sities to dissipation. We must look far-
ther back, not only for the seeds, but
often for the blade and the ear of these
poisonous growths. Their morbid beginnings are to be found, not seldom, very
near the cradle, — by the portals of that
Land of Life where the Ebal and Gerizim
of cursing and blessing stand side by
side. They are in the infantile encour-

agements of inborn depravities. They
are in the senseless gratifications of sensual importunity; in the sweetmeats and
confections of the nursery; in the stimu-
lants and seductions of highly-seasoned
tables; in the nibblings and sippings tolerated by weak or reckless parents, or
by untaught domestics; in all that apparatus and commissary of luxury which
pervert the primal ordinations of nature
in the body, — heat its blood and corrupt its juices, dull the digestion and
quicken the palate, — loosen the muscles
and invigorate the lusts, — disincline to
action, but instigate to pleasure. Thence
come intemperance, gluttony, and un-
chastity. They come of all childish indulgences in eating and drinking. What-

ever theories you may have about drunkenness and the cure of it, — whatever interpretation you may put upon the apostolic recommendation of " *a little* wine for the stomach's sake " of an individual, and that individual probably an invalid, in a wine-producing country, — one thing is clear : the class of persons for whose stomachs, brains, and souls no wine-drinking at all is needful is that of young men in their vigor, young men away from home securities, — such as they may be, — young men amidst convivial exposures, and young men whose business is the use of their minds. Late hours, bad company, mornings of headache, dull recitations, long absence-lists, declining scholarship, complication in crime, broken health, a blighted life, — this is a catalogue of evils which has its real explanation, not on College premises, but in the houses from which the College draws its mixed assemblages; while, on the other hand, those in its walls that carry clear heads and a tender conscience, intellects not sluggish with animal excess, but the flesh made the light and nimble and hardy servitor of the soul, are those who have been taught to keep their bodies under from their childhood, have fought their battle with the imps and demons of the senses long ago, and now scarcely know what the temptation to a surfeit or a carousal means.

In this connection, some reference ought to be made to habits of bodily

3 *

health; for it is manifest — more manifest at present than it used to be — that
neither success, nor happiness, nor usefulness in the scholar is independent of
the physical condition.   Just now, under
the impetus of a fresh enthusiasm, the
muscles are coming to unprecedented
honor.   But it is to be carefully consid-
ered how very unfavorable a spot a College is for the culture, not to say the
repair, of the physical powers.   The student has had too little experience of ill-
ness and pain in his own person to teach
him the dangers that hang about wet
feet, bad ventilation, irregular or solitary
meals, careless changes of clothing, sudden checking of perspiration, lying on
the ground in the intervals of a heating

game of ball, late study by artificial light,
neglect of exercise, and indulgences in
pastry, strong coffee, and tobacco. And
so every class that enters is more or less
thinned, before graduation, by disease;
perhaps by some seated and organic de-
rangement, perhaps by some local dis-
turbance, like weak eyes, or dyspepsia, all
springing from the same general causes.
The two principal safeguards against
these disorders are the energy of a
youthful constitution, which is abundant-
ly relied-upon, and judicious self-regula-
tion, learned as a habit at home. If the
latter is wanting, the risks are fearful
that all the noblest promise and action
of the brain will surrender to inflamed
lungs, or shattered nerves, or an inert

liver, or a fever, before the costly storing up of knowledge has given place to the work of life.

II. A second prevalent source of trouble and failure to the student is insubordination. The moment he joins his class he finds prepared for him a collection of notions embodied in maxims, handed down from one generation to another, about as sacred to a conventional respect as the Mishna and Gemara to the Rabbinical schools, — among which notions are reckoned a natural and necessary hostility of the subject to the government, a disposition to shirk duties, and to regard every law evaded or lesson escaped as a solid gain, — with a regular bias to esteem the hinderance of

an instructor the special prosperity of
the pupil.   Of course, it would be absurd
and wicked to construe these conven-
tions as signs of personal, conscious, and
deliberate ill-will in the young men, who
are commonly gentlemen wholly incapa-
ble of harboring any such feeling, when
taken out of its local connections and
presented as a subject of common sense.
But, notwithstanding, closely connected
with them are many temptations and
acts of real disobedience; violations of
law, occasions of penalty, and thus of
mortification and sorrow.   What is want-
ed is the simple idea of order, an instinct
of our nature, made into a vital principle
applicable to all the relations and management of life, by the patient, steady

c

nurture of parental and domestic discipline.   It belongs *there,* because, being a
principle which often has to grapple and
fight with self-will, it needs to be first un-
folded amidst the gentle and softening
influences of affection, beautified by sym-
pathy, and sanctified by faith.   If first
applied in the colder and more distant
connections between Faculty and pupils,
there must be more or less resistance,
friction, and violence.   It is a principle
that begins to be formed or frustrated
just as soon as the first issue arises between the will of the infant child and
the will of those set over him.   In a
well-governed household, it will be root-
ed and settled, almost past possible re-
consideration, before the academic period

has arrived. Yet who does not see that it is just as much for the comfort and peace of the student as of the officers; that it shuts up a thousand open vexing questions; that it cuts off countless opportunities of collision and regret; that it forestalls the very beginnings of rebellion by a secret decision which forbids the bare thought of it; and that it thus ministers to the common tranquillity of the collegiate body and its members? Indeed, why not extend the same truth to the whole structure of civilized society? It is just here, in the temper of insubordination, — the individual judging the state, the young judging the old, the subject judging the law, and the creature prescribing methods to the Creator, — that we now find one of the radical vices of the commonwealth, of our social manners, and of the Church. Punishments for it are easy enough to invent and apply, under any secure government. But how much better and wiser to instil the obedient and orderly spirit into the very blood and choice of childhood, so that the Home shall both give and receive the blessing !

Why may we not expect, under this more Christian family tutelage, that, instead of a transmitted antagonism, we shall yet see in Universities a transmitted loyalty, — ruler and subject bound together, if not directly by mutual confidence, then at least by a pride and respect for sanctioned authority common to them both, — the interest and honor of the government recognized as the interest and honor of every person governed, — no need of degrading sentences, but only to repronounce, as a watchword, or rallying-cry, the name of that "mother mild," which has become the symbol of liberty and rights, because of duties and of law ?

III. Deserving separate mention, though closely connected with the foregoing, is the danger of self-assertion: a form of selfishness manifested not through the appetites, and less in opposition to the government than to the claims of others, — a blemish on youthful character, and an obstacle to true College success.

4

Young men are quick at reading each other's qualities. Self-seeking has no better prospects there than in the world at large. To make it prosper, even with the transient honors of mortality, and to save it from contempt, it needs extraordinary management. It needs the cunning that knows how to conceal, and the calculation that goes round about. Now these are not apt to be the attributes of the young. Ordinarily they are frank, impulsive, candid. By their peculiar standards, no sort of man is more surely and swiftly disesteemed than he who thrusts into his social intercourse, or his scholastic performances and literary fellowships, the conscious demands of self. See how much, therefore, of the proper joy and nobler satisfaction of his course that student loses altogether who, by being the fondled pet of his parents, the flattered ornament of the household circle, humored even in his most foolish caprices, and coaxed where he ought to be denied, has for his early years a long lesson in egotism and vanity. One of two receptions awaits him, the moment he sets his foot on the College grounds. Either he is forthwith so snubbed and satirized and hustled as to be brought to humbler bearings, has the virus taken out of him, and, by an effectual accession of sense and modesty, gives up the pretension at once of a fop, a " genius," or a prig ; or else, by a special dispensation of good nature, his companions let him alone, and he goes on his way quietly shunned, secretly disliked, abridged of his influence, and of course shortened in his manhood.

Another direction taken by the same sort of conceit is that of a protest against the prescribed methods and established curriculum of the institution. A discovery is made by the lad, that the long experiment of learned men, who for generations have given their lives to the matter, has somehow missed the practical point; and so, instead of making up his mind to use the apparatus, instruction, library, and cabinet, for the express purpose assigned, and for which he or his friends must pay so much time and money, he shirks the regular studies, sets up an image of general belles-lettres reputation or thrilling eloquence, reads poetry and the reviews, attends the societies, counts it a special piece of wit to despise the sciences and classics, and puts himself into an attitude of general criticism, if not compassion, towards the particular objects and industries of the place. Possibly he undertakes the "mission" of a "reformer of all work," and enlists in philanthropic endeavors to rectify the policy of the College, when he ought to be learning its lessons. Now, for these cases,——which are not common, but which occur,——there is no proper remedy in the collegiate instruction. The remedy, which is rather a preventive, lies in those plastic periods when every child

4 *

should learn his place, be shown the honor and decorum of respecting his superiors and obeying their rules. If this is slighted in its season, the retribution is parental mortification at a wasted or a suddenly terminated College career.

IV. The intellectual form of selfishness is emulative ambition: a radical disorder in our schools and our scholarship. Let me tell you what I have seen in our Christian New England; — two brilliant, high-hearted youths, the rival leaders of their class, all the rest left behind, stretching across the four years' course neck and neck, stimulated by the spur of an eager emulation, sacrificing health and peace, only to drop, one into a grave and the other into mental perversion, at

the end of the heat : this instead of that
nobler spectacle, — both striving gener-
ously together for wisdom's own immortal and unbounded good, each rejoicing
in the other's gains, and then both standing, nay, kneeling rather, gratefully together on the summit both have reached.
We put our pupils too much on this race,
not that they may attain a common
good, but that they may outstrip each
other. To be wise, to be strong, to be
masters of life, wielders of bright weap-
ons against all ignorance and wrong, —
this is not made the aim, — but the poor
complacency of looking back on the rest.
A hateful fire is set running through the
fresh growths of these unsordid breasts,
which scorches, blights, and blackens,

wherever its hot tongue can find a generous feeling to singe. Paint me, said the boy Chatterton, to an artist who asked for a design, — paint me an angel with trumpet and wings, to publish my name over the world! Plagiarism, madness, suicide, were the horrible chapters of his biography. Why talk of following knowledge for its own sake, if our practice teaches children to prize it only as a ladder to renown, or as a price paid for applause? But, my friends, the moment you carry your objections to the conductors of education, they tell you the emulative plan is the only one that the previous management of their scholars allows them to use, with the least hope of getting out of them any tolerable amount of work. That is to say, the trail of the serpent runs all the way from alphabet to diploma : — and who knows how far beyond ? Prior once proposed a system of early education, by having sweet-cakes cut out in the shape of the letters, — the child to eat a letter' as soon as he had learned it, and so on, till he had devoured and digested this baked alphabet. One is reminded of this philosophy of compound nourishment, when he sees children made to believe that the only purpose of learning is to be fattened, whether on cake, money, or compliments. Suppose rather that, from the beginning of his studies, the boy were made to feel that the grand object of them is usefulness to society and the service of God. Suppose the question put foremost by the voice of father and mother, teachers and companions, were, how to learn to contribute the largest life to the welfare of man, and so how to help others to live; how to lighten the load of the wronged and oppressed; how to raise burdens, and cheer outcasts, and render science the minister to overtasked strength, and turn discovery to the relief of sorrow : —

> " How best to help the slender store,
> How mend the dwellings of the poor,
> How gain in life, as life advances,
> Valor and Charity, more and more."

The mind can never open into its largest compass and power under any but the broadest and highest motives. Nor can we begin too soon to expand it by that Christian measure.

V. In some degree at variance with the danger of a selfish ambition, and yet often trying to keep it company, is that of an inordinate passion for popularity : the more seductive because it often joins itself with dispositions and manners intrinsically attractive. I hold that the acquiring and cultivating of some genial and lasting friendships is one of the right objects of College life. Popularity, sought for power, is only another kind of ambition. Popularity, sought for the mere social currency, the luxury of pleasing and being pleased, and the excitement of the spirits, is a humaner

thing.   Yet, the moment it passes the
Christian limit, it becomes a weakness,
weakening true manliness. It has its
own pernicious alliances, and works its
own mischiefs. While ambition insti-
gates to greater application, the love
of popularity is quite as likely to run
to idleness. While the former by its
intellectual element may keep a man
out of conviviality, this is always liable
to drag him into it. Its worst conse-
quences are compromises of conscience;
yieldings of that stern and lofty principle which is the only certain glory of a
man; the fatal downfall of a righteous
independence; the fear to stand up
bravely for a conviction, and to stand
alone for it, to the life's end; the calling

of good evil, and evil good; the winking
at falsehoods, or other sins, as trivial,
only because Satan has made them fash-
ionable. Not that there are no examples
found among young men of an upright-
ness all the more popular for its fearless-
ness, especially if without cant or mo-
roseness. Still, these must always be, in
College as in the rest of the world, the
illustrious exceptions. For the most
part, the temptations and the favor-
seekers go together; and the man who
is determined to have "a good time," at
all hazards, finds enough others glad of
his countenance, his pocket-money, and
his flattery. Now, what are all these
supple compliances but the ripened pro-
duct of the same misdirected inclinations

which, years ago, slid away from the
parents into the kitchen, to catch up the
smooth gossip, coaxing, and adulation of
the servants, or strolled into the street to
find a laxer and gayer companionship;
or, on the ball-ground, took the side of
the majority against that inflexible fellow
that dared to be singular, or the un-
popular one that was so unfortunate as
to be born awkward, or taciturn, or
poor? What right have you to presume
the twist of seventeen years shall be
straightened and forgot, by a transfer
from your own roof to the crowded and
unwatched walls of the College?

VI. A more honest kinswoman of this
relish of popularity is genuine kindliness
of heart; — that blessed and brightening

grace which redeems a community of
young or old from barbarism, — is the
charm of politeness, the cordiality of
manners, the very essence of friendship,
and, next to piety toward God, the
purest manifestation of Christian love.
You may suppose that, in the careless
and happy groups which move through
the walks and share the pleasures of academic retreats, no darker and maligner
spirit need ever intrude. And were all
parents Christian parents, and all Christian parents faithful, and the Church con-
sistent, so it might be. Sourness and bit-
terness, malice and envying, slander and
revenge, cruelty and scorn, would surely
seem to have no invitation or natural
admission in these equalized and inti-

mate companies, where prejudice, and party, and mammon have no rightful foothold. But there is no fence about a College to bar out the transgressions of human kind. There is no sieve to winnow away the fostered iniquities of the candidates that come in. It is no Delos of inevitable peace. Your sons will bring the unfeeling temper that bad control has packed in their hearts, as surely as the raiment that your providence has packed in their trunks. They will find some foolish fashions, half inhumanity and half fun, the mixed heirloom of spite and sport, all ready to their hands. Whether they shall disown the barbarous inheritance ; whether they shall reject the petty tyranny, and keep

the harmless frolic; whether they shall
be bullies and boors and pugilists on the
playground, or gentlemen everywhere;
whether they shall count their fellows'
feelings as sacred, and as deserving to
be as delicately heeded, and their sen-
sibilities to be as scrupuiously respected,
as any rights of purse or rank; whether
they shall magnanimously mark every
sensitive nature, or sensitive spot in a
harder nature, so as not to torture, but to
encourage and reassure and comfort it;
in short, whether they shall play the part
of malevolence or mercy, Christ's men or
devil's men; — do you not believe this is
all to be chiefly decided before they ever
take the first classmate by the hand?

In order to cure the worst abuses we

have among us, we want a more liberal infusion of this royal, manly gentleness. Join it with what vivacity, or wit, or robust laughter, you will ; only pour it in upon us, in the hearts of your boys, and you will Christianize our lingering savageness faster than by statutes, or corporation votes, or public denunciation. Let me tell you a story, not vouching for its particulars, but as it was told to me. You all know what "hazing" is, — and how threadbare and flat its ever repeated acts of silly violence have come to be. They say that not long ago some Sophomores, of better purpose and more humor than some of their predecessors, heard that two Freshmen in their building were fighting poverty for an education. One cold winter night, rapping loudly at their door, the Sophomores called them up, ordered them to dress, and led them up stairs blindfold to a distant room. Leaving them there for their comrades to entertain, they then returned to the bare and empty room, spread a comfortable carpet over the floor, packed the closet full of fuel, built a roaring fire in the grate, made things generally cheerful, led back the bewildered Freshmen to their own door, shoved them in, and bade them good night. This is "hazing" gone philanthropic. A very few such spirited jets of good feeling would revolutionize the stupidest custom that disgraces us. I have made no inquiry; but nobody here will doubt that the prophecy of this little gospel might have been easily traced in two or three cheerful, kindly, charitable homes. God multiply them!

Seek out the families where the children are suffered to plague each other, to impose on the younger, to despotize over timid servants, or to vex animals and murder insects, and you will be sure to find the material that will stock a University with brutes. Seek the homes of happy, free-hearted charity, and you will find the antidote that will at last turn brutality itself into goodness. For, remember, in this as in other respects we have noticed, it is not the ascetic, forbidding discipline, not the gloomy or sharp-strung households, that send us the right trusty hearts and consciences. These only prepare a reaction, and let their children loose, when they send them from home, into the wild excesses of license.

VII. These allusions bring us on to the last and profoundest condition of the student's welfare, honor and success,— his religious reverence and faith. Whatever may be thought of the views foregoing, I am sure no parent here, who has ever come to pray that his child may believe and fear God and keep his commandments, will deny that the divinely appointed school for this heavenly nurture is "the Church in the House." No later care, however vigilant or fortified, can make up for the terrible mischief of one irreligious year in childhood. No provisions of teaching or example, by a College government, can heal the ghastly wound inflicted by a father's profanity. No theory of heavenly grace can excuse the Christian mother from her holy offices, serving in Christ's ministry. What was testified by one of the strong statesmen of our early American history might be confessed in substance, probably, by nearly all the best men that have lived in Christendom. "I believe," he said, "that I should have been swept away by the flood of French infidelity, but for one thing, — the remembrance of the time when my sainted mother used to make me kneel by her bedside, taking my little hands folded in hers, and causing me to repeat the Lord's prayer." I have been told that, in the wonderful and gracious experiments made in our times for kindling up a little light even in the darkness of idiocy, the first ray of intelligence that is observed to gleam across the imbecile's vacant face, and the first pulse of feeling strong enough to overmaster furious passions and arrest the aimless eyes, commonly appear when some gentle touch or tone of womanly kindness rekindles in the heart the flickering impressions of a mother's tenderness. Could any proof more striking show us what lips, whose countenance, ought first to dedicate the child to the Holy One? Even the old Romans in their heathenism had a touching superstition of holding the face of the new-born infant upward to the heavens, signifying, by thus presenting his forehead to the stars, that he was to look above the world, into glories celestial. The goddess that was supposed to preside over this aspiring ceremony was named from a word which means "to raise aloft." A superstition it was then. Christianity, dispelling the fable and the doubt, gives us the clear realization of the dim, Pagan yearning, in a Christian baptism and the training of the Fold. What shall be said of those nominally Christian parents who discover less than the heathen sensibility, and, with all the blessed ordinances of the Divine Son of Mary in their sight, refuse to their children even the covenant and benediction of the Church ?

There is a fable, in German literature, of the daughter of an Erl-King, whose infernal business it is to snatch little children away from parents and home. She comes even into the parents' presence, and there, with crafty disguises and fair appearance, deceiving them in her malignant purpose, she contrives to whisper into the unsuspecting ears many artful promises of fine shows and happy plays, till at last she wiles away victim after victim into dreary forests, — the land of darkness and shadows of death. Do we not all know something of this child-thief's seductions? Temptation is the Erl-King's daughter that never dies. She tears away children from their Father's House, — from virtue, from peace, from heaven.   And you, parents, all help her or hinder her.   If you are doing everything else for them, in expenditure and accomplishment, save only that one thing without which all the rest is worthless, you are giving them up already to despair.   If you make them in infancy only the sentimental recreation and pampered fondlings of your idle hours, or send them out into the streets bespread with the fineries and fopperies of your own vanity, you will make them, not noble members of a high-bred state, but only the possible heirs of your property, and drivelling exhibitions of the accursed thirst for pomp and dress which debilitates our civilization and impoverishes our humanity.   If you take up the

unbelieving and abominable theory, that
all children have got to run wild awhile,
in the ways of corruption and vice, tast-
ing death, before they can be gathered
into the securities of religion, then you
are training them to be disciples of that
bleak creed, life without a faith, home
without a Saviour, learning without a
Bible. Somewhere, by some tongue,
your child must be reverently taught in
Christ's Gospel, or the wisest systems can
promise you nothing for him. Not by
chance, not at interrupted and infrequent
seasons, but patiently and humbly, and
day by day, that wonderful, most an-
cient and eternal Book of books must
be opened before him. Its sublime yet
simple truths, plain to the child's under-

standing, its hallowed personages, its grand prophets and ardent apostles, its venerable patriarchs and its inspired children, in their robes of light and forms of majesty and beauty, must pass before him. Its psalms must be sung into his soul. Its beatitudes and warnings must be planted in his remembrance. Its parables must engage his fancy. Its miracles must stir his wonder. Its cross, and tabernacle, and ark, and all its sacred emblems, must people his imagination and possess his heart. Without that Bible, no child born among us can "pass the waves of this troublesome world," and come to Him whom only the Bible reveals.

But regard your offspring as the lawful inheritors, through you, of Christ's spiritual covenants, as the destined members of his Church, and imitators of his life, and partakers of his redemption, as the appointed subjects of baptism, of prayer, of inward renewing and outward regulation, — as being born, each one, to yield the world a Christian character, and thus as being fearfully wronged whenever religious indifference cheats them of this immortal privilege, — do this, and you will have no occasion to run in search of honors or favors for them. Do this, and in all our scholarship, society, and enterprise the kingdom of Heaven will come in the natural way, handed down from parent to child in the blood and all the hereditary strength of believing generations, spreading and gaining power with all the growth and progress and wisdom and refinement of the race.

Such, my patient friends, seem to me some of the points of practical connection between the life lived in our Colleges, and the moral culture of our Homes. It may seem to you that, in illustrating them, I have presented rather the aspects of danger than those of hope. Let me earnestly assure you, then, that this has been only for the sake of giving emphasis to the pressing importance of the subject.

As to the mere question of fact, I join in no alarm. Such opportunities of judgment as I happen to have had in both lead me to the belief that, as respects

moral perils and exposures, there is but
little to choose between the college community and that of any equal number
of young men collected, or even scat-
tered, in any central population, away
from home ; and perhaps I might even
say, whether away from home or not.
There are some special safeguards, perhaps, at the College, in the routine of
tasks, the frequency of the exercises, the
pressure of occupation, and the general
direction of the preparatory course. It
so happens, in this neighborhood, that
nearly every delinquency of undergrad-
uates above the breaking of a window-
pane is chronicled for the public, and
reported over the country, till the opin-
ion has become quite prevalent, that any

young man who gets his degree without
becoming a bully, an atheist, or a sot,
escapes by about one chance in ten. The
truth is, the large majority in every College are the quiet, industrious students,
of whom the public hears nothing till
they begin to be public men, coming up
from virtuous and orderly houses, know-
ing perfectly well what they have come
for, and pursuing their object steadily,
worthily, and virtuously. Circumstances
are less unlike than they seem, and are
hardly ever too mighty for a man. Principle is safe everywhere, for the Almighty
is with it. The good conscience carries
its own shield. The prayers of youth
" prevail as a prince ; " and the interces-
sions of any " household of faith " sur-

round the absent son and brother with invisible power like a legion of angels.

Indeed, the very truth presented here is full of encouragement. It discloses the whole formation of character, from first to last, as held under fixed and intelligible laws. We are not left for confidence in our children's security to the blind and forlorn impulses of accident, but with a God and Father who remembers his covenants. Some strange, sad instances of a surprising lapse, or revolution into ruin, may distress us still. But, for the most part, thanks to the Lord and Redeemer of families, believing parents may build on a sure foundation, and, with a religious nurture in childhood, look for the faith afterward which overcometh the world.

When the Christian Home and the Christian College are thus bound together, each a helper and minister to the other, the grandest expectations of our fathers may be fulfilled. Education may then train, not portions and fragments of our nature, but the whole character and life of man. It may equip the lawgivers and teachers and priests and citizens of a righteous and holy state. Learning may be humane, labor enlightened, commerce disinterested, art pure, the Church catholic, and the republic the kingdom of Christ.

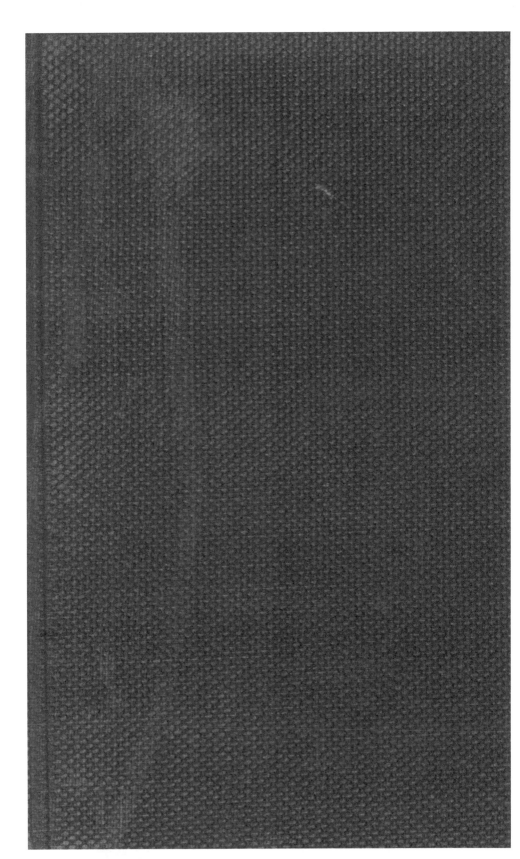

Check Out More Titles From HardPress Classics Series In this collection we are offering thousands of classic and hard to find books. This series spans a vast array of subjects – so you are bound to find something of interest to enjoy reading and learning about.

Subjects:
Architecture
Art
Biography & Autobiography
Body, Mind &Spirit
Children & Young Adult
Dramas
Education
Fiction
History
Language Arts & Disciplines
Law
Literary Collections
Music
Poetry
Psychology
Science
…and many more.

Visit us at www.hardpress.net

CPSIA information can be obtained
at www.ICGtesting.com
Printed in the USA
BVHW042323110819
555626BV00017B/4725/P